Hell at Cock's Crow

Hell at Cock's Crow

Poems by

Robert Cooperman

© 2023 Robert Cooperman. All rights reserved.
This material may not be reproduced in any form, published,
reprinted, recorded, performed, broadcast,
rewritten or redistributed without
the explicit permission of Robert Cooperman.
All such actions are strictly prohibited by law.

Cover design by Shay Culligan

ISBN: 978-1-63980-467-2

Kelsay Books
502 South 1040 East, A-119
American Fork, Utah 84003
Kelsaybooks.com

As Always, for Beth, my Pirate Queen

Acknowledgments

The author wishes to thank the editors of the journals listed below, where some of these poems, sometimes in earlier form, were first published.

Blue Unicorn: "Captain James Raven Closes on the Merchantman, *The Peacock*"

The Flying Dodo: "Captain James Raven Considers Kathleen Munro"

The Lyric: "The Merchantman's Cook, Hiding in the Hold," "Philip Farr, Able Bodied Seaman and Pirate," "Samuel Wallace, Ship's Cook, Still Hiding from Pirates"

Contents

The Pirate's Oath — 15

PART I—THE TAKING OF *THE PEACOCK*

Pirate Captain James Raven Closes on
   The Merchantman, *The Peacock* — 19
The Merchantman's Cook — 20
Captain Abraham Martin of *The Peacock*,
   About to Be Killed by Pirates — 21
Captain James Raven, After Captain Abraham
   Martin Leaps into the Sea — 22
Billy Butcher, Late an Able-Bodied Seaman of
   The Peacock, a New Pirate — 23
Billy Butcher Considers Life as a Pirate — 24

PART II—HIDE AND SEEK

The Merchantman's Cook, Hiding in the Hold — 27
Philip Farr, Able Bodied Seaman and Pirate — 28
Captain James Raven Speaks of His Crew — 29
Samuel Wallace, Ship's Cook, as the Number of
   Pirates He Kills Grows — 30
Samuel Wallace, Still Hiding from Pirates — 31
Billy Butcher Thinks of Samuel Wallace — 32
Samuel Wallace Thinks of Billy Butcher — 33
Weeks Later, Captain Raven Orders *The Peacock*
   Burned — 34
Matthew Steyne, Second in Command to Captain
   Raven — 35
The Ship's Cook, About to Leave *The Peacock* — 36
The Governor — 37

PART III—A FLY IN THE OINTMENT

Billy Butcher Makes Plans to Leave the Pirate Life	41
A Fly in the Ointment of Billy Butcher's Plans to Escape	42
The Pirate Kathleen Munro Thinks of Billy Butcher	43
The Reluctant Pirate Billy Butcher Thinks Further on Kathleen	44
The Pirate Kathleen Munro Thinks Further on Billy Butcher	45
Kathleen Munro, on How She Was Drawn into the Pirate Life by Captain James Raven	46
The Pirate Kathleen Munro Talks About Captain Raven	47
Kathleen Munro Thinks Further About Captain Raven	48
Captain James Raven Considers Kathleen Munro	49
The Pirate Kathleen Munro Further Vacillates About Leaving	50
Kathleen Munro Thinks of Miranda Iglesias	51
Miranda Iglesias, Consort of Captain Raven	52
How Miranda Iglesias Became a Pirate	53
How Miranda Iglesias Became a Pirate, II	54
How Miranda Iglesias First Proved Her Mettle as a Pirate	55
Miranda Iglesias, on Gaining the Attention of James Raven	56
Captain Raven Remembers His First and Only Slave Ship	57
James Raven Rationalizes Sending Captured Crewmen into Indentured Servitude	58

Captain Raven Remembers His First Pirate Command	59
Samuel Wallace Continues to Assassinate James Raven's Pirate Crew	60

PART IV—THE GOVERNOR

Why the Governor Assumed His Posting	63
The Governor's Business Arrangements	64
The Governor, on the Climate of the Islands	65
The Governor Thinks of His Mistress	66
Eliza Townes Thinks of Her Paramour, the Governor	67
The Governor Explains Why He Hasn't Sent Troops to Take the Pirate Stronghold	68

PART V—CAPTURE

Kathleen Munro Changes Her Mind About the Pirate Life	71
The Governor, Ready to Attack the Pirate Stronghold	72
Billy Butcher and Kathleen Munro Escape	73
The Governor Deploys His Forces Against the Pirate Stronghold	74
Too Late, Pirate James Raven Discovers the Desertion of Billy Butcher and Kathleen Munro	75
Captured, James Raven Voices His Regrets	76

PART VI—HELL AT COCK'S CROW

The Governor, Before the Execution of James Raven	79
James Raven Addresses the Vicar at His Hanging	80
James Raven's Final Words to the Hangman	81
The Hangman Converses with James Raven on the Scaffold	82
Samuel Wallace at the Hanging of James Raven	83
Miranda Iglesias, in the Crowd at James Raven's Hanging	84
The Governor to His Lieutenant, at the Hanging of James Raven	85
Miranda Iglesias Tries to Escape from the Governor's Henchman	86
Taken Prisoner by the Governor, Miranda Iglesias Makes the Best of Things	87
Miranda Iglesias Plans Her Escape	88
Miranda Iglesias Rids Herself of the Governor	89

EPILOGUE—ON THE SEA AND BEYOND

Billy Butcher and Kathleen Munro, on the Sea	93
Miranda Iglesias Returns to the Pirate Life	94
Billy Butcher and Kathleen Munro Make Landfall	95
Kathleen Munro, After the Birth of Her and Billy's Butcher Son	96
Billy Butcher, Five Years After His Pirate Adventures Have Ended	97
Miranda Iglesias Has the Last Word	98

The Pirate's Oath

Fat, comfortable men sneer we're Hell's blooms,
Satan's foul droppings, foes to all mankind,
fit only to be hunted, necks and spines
wishbone broken by the hangman at noon,

when the most boisterous crowd is gathered
to witness and cheer, victuals and drinks sold
for a profit by enterprising souls,
our corpses gibbet-caged; then bones scattered

or crossroads-buried, for all to trample,
a plaque stating, "Here lies one forever damned,
a brigand on the sea, a doomed man.
May his sufferings below be ample."

Fools, there's only this one life for us all.
Heaven? Hell? Pictures fading on a wall.

PART I—THE TAKING OF *THE PEACOCK*

"Explore the ship!
Replace the cook!
Let no one leave alive!"

—Keith Reid and Gary Booker,
"A Salty Dog"

Pirate Captain James Raven Closes on The Merchantman, *The Peacock*

"Prepare a broadside, you scurvy sea-hounds!"
I boomed out, loud as a six-pounder. "Fire!"
Shells more tuneful than Handel's *Messiah,*
to render *The Peacock*'s sails into shrouds,

leaving the hull intact for us to board
and claim the ship, after minor repairs,
while we secure her treasures and wares,
though deck-blood's a shallow stream to ford

once we're on the ship, rounding up her crew
"Make certain you find the ship's cook!" I call,
"the bastard will want to poison us all,
deceiving us with his sweet-smelling stew."

"And bring the captain to stand before me,
to take our oath or dumped into the sea."

The Merchantman's Cook

Lurking in the shadow-shield of a cove,
the pirate cur fired its broadside big-guns,
ripped our sails before we could make a run,
boarded us for rumors of gems and gold.

I knew I had to hide, always the cook
the first of all the crew to sink or float
to cheers, or a slashing blade to the throat,
for they know I'd be ruthless as a rook

in poisoning the bastards' food rations.
But unlike that dark bird of tearing death,
I'd be silent as snow on winter earth,
men puking-dead at their watchful stations.

I keep an empty barrel in the hold
for this purpose, to sneak from, dagger-bold.

Captain Abraham Martin of *The Peacock,*
About to Be Killed by Pirates

The pox-mad wretches made me stand and stare
while they lined up and butchered all my crew,
cauldroned the ship's deck into a blood stew:
slaughter worse than the handiwork of bears.

Of course they saved me for last, hoped the wait
would turn my legs to aspic, make me plead
for mercy on my supplicating knees
at their taunts that I'd soon be mere shark bait

now that the beady-eyed monsters have gathered
in their impatience to make a feast of me
with my men festering in the beasts' bellies,
they turn the sea to a bloody lather.

I'll give these sea rats not a jot of pleasure,
but will stroll the plank with an earl's leisure.

Captain James Raven, After Captain Abraham Martin Leaps into the Sea

The stupid bugger's own fault he ventured
past the cove where my ship lurked, to waylay
fat, cargo-rich merchantmen on their way
up the coast; we sell crews as indentured

slaves in the Colonies, if they don't fight.
If they do, we put them all to the sword,
heave their bloody carcasses overboard,
punishment for resisting, not for spite.

But first, we give them a chance to join us,
to become part of our democracy
and rove and pillage on the wild blue sea.
But most of them refused in a chorus.

Now, their captain swaggers his stately path
on the plank, I smile, knowing the sharks' wrath.

Billy Butcher, Late an Able-Bodied Seaman of *The Peacock,* a New Pirate

I didn't sign on to be turned into chum
for sharks and such, by murdering sea dogs
raiding our hold quicker than hungry hogs
after they boarded us, the filthy scum.

So when their captain asked, "Who'll join our crew?"
I stepped forward, though my former shipmates
muttered, "Coward, turncoat; God's sealed your fate!"
"No," I hissed, "I'll not trade places with you

when these lads nudge you into the drink
at sword-point. Look what awaits you below.
If you're so sure of Heaven at cock-crow
you'd not find a way to step back from death's brink."

"Even if it meant sailing with these wolves?
Life too fleeting to be a righteous fool."

Billy Butcher Considers Life as a Pirate

Not so different from other ships I've signed
on for, though we sleep, drink, fight, and fuck more,
wenches aplenty in buccaneer ports
well-hidden from the King, and fortified

with cannons: the bays sabotaged with mines.
No marines to lay the cat to your back,
though I've seen men hanged, their faces crow-black
after Jack Ketch strung them from his hemp line,

placed them in gibbets, for rooks' beaks and taunts.
A rope, that's how I'll end, sooner or late,
by our captain's fickle hand, or the State's;
we're nothing but pawns, mice, hunted with scorn.

The consolation, while my luck holds fast,
are the clink of coins, the moans of a lass.

PART II—HIDE AND SEEK

The Merchantman's Cook, Hiding in the Hold

From the keg where I hide I try to hear
the pirates; my crew, I silently cried,
have been butchered and shoved over the side:
none blessed with Our Dear Lord's salvation prayer.

So when all is silent, with just the squeak
of rats, the shifting of ballast-barrels,
the ship's rise and fall in the troughs and swells,
when all I can hear are the beams creak,

it's then I creep out of my bolt hole,
lift some food, *my* food, from *my* ship's galley,
sneak on deck as if a harbor alley
and quietly send a black hearted, thieving soul

down to the bottom of Satan's dark sea,
the bastard cursed for all eternity.

Philip Farr, Able Bodied Seaman and Pirate

I knew we should've let *The Peacock* be,
not shot out her mainsail and boarded her,
then rounded up her crew and did murder
on them, their hides tossed to the hungry sea.

Now one of their ghosts, maybe more than one,
stalks us like a shark in the fog of night,
killing us all with a dirk or with fright:
bodies slipping below, before the sun

can rise and turn that spirit into stone,
so we might at least see our killer's face
though too late to grant us that one small grace,
for he's air and mist, not dead flesh and bones.

Captain Raven curses our quaking terror;
mocking us will be his gravest error.

Captain James Raven Speaks of His Crew

What a credulous litter of scoundrels
my crew has turned out to be, chattering
their terror about a ghost splattering
their shipmates' bodies over the gunwales,

their corpses gnawed by the beasts of the sea.
The fools: a dead man's spirit's not to blame,
but a cur we failed to catch at his game
of quiet vengeance; so far he's killed three

of my men, and soon no one left but me,
whom he'll take last, letting me shit my britches;
the fellow's a brazen son of a bitch,
the craftiest bastard on the salt sea.

I've sent my men to hunt him in the hold;
I'll slash him with steel for being so bold.

Samuel Wallace, Ship's Cook, as the Number of Pirates He Kills Grows

I fear I grow too fond of taking the lives
of the brutes who murdered *The Peacock*'s crew.
I wasn't suckled on a devil's brew
of killing, and so many more still alive:

so many, I can't count them, let alone
take retribution on each. I weary,
too, of skulking in the hold: dank, dreary,
with rats chattering, nipping at my bones.

I can crawl out only at night, to lurk
in shadows and waylay another scum
reeling from his tot-ful and more of rum,
send him to Satan with my deadly dirk.

Still, some had no choice: "Join our pirate larks
or we'll toss you to schools of circling sharks."

Samuel Wallace, Still Hiding from Pirates

Four pirate curs I've sent to hell so far,
foggy nights serving as a cloak for me
while I partake of vengeful butchery,
though the swine grow wary under the stars.

Less likely to grow besotted with grog
and make an easy mark for my swift blade,
they walk hunched over, listening, afraid,
though I'm silent, fatal as Black-Death fog.

So far the fools haven't scented my lair
in a dark corner of the dripping hold,
nor have they caught me when I make so bold
to climb to the deck and breathe the sweet salt air.

But only a wee time before they do;
at least I'll have avenged some of my crew.

Billy Butcher Thinks of Samuel Wallace

When I turned pirate rather than amble
off the plank, prodded by a sea-dog's dirk,
I knew that Wallace, *The Peacock*'s cook, lurked
below decks somewhere, waiting to scramble

out during the night-watch, to slash and stab
this thieving crew. Captain Raven told me
to take a bloodthirsty company,
"To search the hold and kill the whoreson-scab!"

But I couldn't: instead, pretended to trip,
so the noise would forewarn Wallace to hide
in a new bolt hole, and there to abide
'til we were drunk on the deck of the ship.

'Tis a perilous game I play at sea,
Raven mistrusting my loyalty.

Samuel Wallace Thinks of Billy Butcher

So far, Butcher, that turncoat pirate-scum,
hasn't given away my hiding places
to the rats who slaughtered our crew: faces
I'll be haunted by until Kingdom Come.

When he leads his brother-filth below-decks
to find and haul me before this Raven—
who calls himself their leader, their captain,
though he's merely a treacherous fly-speck

I'd like to step on—Butcher will always
make a subtle dry cough or thud or scrape
of a heel, to give me time to escape
into a new bolt-hole; still, he'd betray

me, if it helped to preserve his own skin.
But grudgingly, thus far, I must thank him.

Weeks Later, Captain Raven Orders *The Peacock* Burned

The Devil take that treacherous Jack Tar
who nightly emerges to kill my crew,
though we've scoured the ship 'til we've all turned blue,
combed high and low, up and down, near and far.

Not an inch of the hold has gone un-searched,
he's made fools of us all; even worse,
trembles my men into thinking they're cursed
for killing his mates, as if saints in church!

Not a crate or keg's still left in the hold,
they've been pried open for a hiding place,
but he's nowhere, not a mist or a trace
of that ghost, to drag him to our scaffold.

So it's time to flush the rat out with fire,
or watch his stave-and-pitch funeral pyre.

Matthew Steyne, Second in Command to Captain Raven

You ask me, the Raven's gone croaking daft:
wanting to burn *The Peacock* merchantman we took,
to flush out their roving, murderous cook,
who stalks the deck with deadly, dagger craft.

Sell the ship, I keep telling him, make it
some simpleton captain and crew's concern.
For all we know, that cook is long gone; burn-
ing Her will just set fire to our profits.

As for the knifings that still bleed the night?
Most likely, the crew settling dirty scores;
men less trustworthy than poxy whores.
They'd kill their Ma's over the slightest slight.

But the Raven's deaf to my good advice;
better, had he been tranced by rum and dice.

The Ship's Cook, About to Leave *The Peacock*

These pirate-scum think they've searched every foot
of the hold, emptied every keg and cask,
pried loose boards, reeling from flagons and flasks
of rum; and find just mouse droppings and soot,

while staggering past my sanctuary.
In the dark dog-watch, I'm an assassin,
moving knife-silent, to avenge the men
I sailed with from here to the Irrawaddy.

The ship docked near shore, I'll stalk from my hole
one last time, and find a snoring brigand,
slide my blade between his ribs soft as sand,
then slip into the sea black as a mole,

and swim ashore: time to leave this ghost ship
and its hell-crew, and give these curs the slip.

The Governor

My spies tell me an angel's been afoot
in the hold of the pirate-held *Peacock,*
so that Raven, that sea-scum, shat rocks
of terror when evening darkened to soot

and shadows grew long, then vanished in night,
and every sound could be an assassin
stalking him or one of his wretched men,
depriving me justice from a rope's height.

Still, I applaud the killer's sacred work,
though Raven has moved his vile crew ashore,
where they revel with rum and poxy whores,
but still there's the fear an avenger lurks

in dark corners with a butchering blade,
to make those bastards jump at every shade.

PART III—A FLY IN THE OINTMENT

Billy Butcher Makes Plans to Leave the Pirate Life

The King's high-governor will track us down,
bid us stand upon his Master's gallows,
our corpses tossed into creaking wheelbarrows;
and that will be the end of this sea hound,

'less I take a gamer's chance, and depart
at some safe port, steal a wind-loving skiff;
a night-sail to the mainland's worth the risk,
to forsake the sea forever, and start

a new, honest life in the Colonies
and forget I ever was a pirate,
though forced into that scoundrel's thieving fate:
my choice: death or a life of butchery.

I've had enough of pillage, blood, and rape.
If my scurvy crewmates blink, I'll escape.

A Fly in the Ointment of Billy Butcher's Plans to Escape

What to do about that sweet bawd Kathleen,
with her soft breasts, hot quim, and flaming mane?
If I confide my plan, she might betray
me to Captain Raven, to make herself queen

of his heart and move up the great chain
of scoundrels, and rule this scummy island
with him; me nothing more than her wee, bland,
temporary rung before she can claim

her exalted place in this demon-kingdom.
Still, I bless my luck each time she takes me
between her legs, my insides quivering jelly,
my raptures as near as I'll get to heaven.

Each time we do the dirty, lovely deed,
I think that, maybe, this is all I need.

The Pirate Kathleen Munro Thinks of Billy Butcher

After the Raven gave the toy to me—
Billy sensibly joining us rather
than make shark chum—I was ordered to gather
as much about him as I could, to see

if he meant to stay true to us, or run
at the first chance he could seize, and turn rat
to the Governor, for a reward fat
as this lazy, tropical noonday sun.

I could sense he plans to leave us, not mated
to the pirate life, priggish about killing,
holding back when it came to blood-spilling
when we overran soft merchantmen fated

to fall. But the Governor's canary?
He just wants to be far away and free.

The Reluctant Pirate Billy Butcher Thinks Further on Kathleen

Maybe if I tell her my plans, she'll fly
this pirate's nest with me, swear she loves me
and me alone, keep me from catastrophes,
with her darting dagger, and loving eye.

Boyo, you're blinded with a madman's love;
she was given to you by Captain Raven,
her loyalty first and only to him,
the pretty talons in his iron glove.

Still, a man can hope that love does run true,
or that it's more than her just taking orders
to sniff out my plans, so she can report
to Raven, who'll stand me before the crew

and have me stretched, poked, and pierced endlessly,
while sweet Kathleen smirks at my agony.

The Pirate Kathleen Munro Thinks Further on Billy Butcher

He is a sweet piece, enthusiastic:
nuzzling and grateful after we're spent, lying
side by sweaty side, but I know he's dying
to confide—while we're sated, soft, and slick

with love's juices—he wants to leave our hive,
to find lawful work at sea or on land,
but if he places himself in my hands
he knows I'm naught but Captain Raven's spy.

Still, I'll mourn to watch him swing or get shoved
into the shark-circling sea; it's too daft
a risk to sail with him in a stolen craft.
Much as I'd like that sweet dream and would love

to tie myself to his side, I can't see
hard farm toil or a fishwife reek for me.

Kathleen Munro, on How She Was Drawn into the Pirate Life by Captain James Raven

I'd always dreamed of a life on the sea,
to squirrel-dash up and down the rat-lines,
better than the tumbler's trade any time:
the kiss of winds blowing salty and free.

So I stole off from home, dressed as a boy,
bound my budding breasts, cropped my girlish hair,
pitched my voice lower, and took special care
none espied me squatting to piss, all coy.

But we were boarded by some pirate scum;
they gave us the choice of joining their crew
or be tossed into the midst of a slew
of sharks boiling the water, like a scrum.

The Raven gave me one hard, smirking glance,
then dragged me below and tore off my pants.

The Pirate Kathleen Munro Talks About Captain Raven

When Captain Bastard Raven took me below,
he didn't let me off his bed for days,
my body thrumming, heart a precious vase:
he'd bewitched me in his private bagnio.

"I've a special job for you," his smile sly,
after I was a glad slave to his will,
for the way he made me float, soar, and thrill.
"You'll be my eyes and ears, my pretty spy.

"Men will open up like roses to you,
for you'll stoke their self-esteem like a fire,
flatter them their wee pricks are church spires,
that they deserve their own ships, their own crews."

I would've pledged him my life, anything:
for the way he made me shimmer and sing

Kathleen Munro Thinks Further About Captain Raven

He made it plain I'd never be his queen,
just his ruthless, efficient courtier,
his secret weapon, his hidden rapier,
so cunning, clever, deadly and keen.

At first I thought I could sweeten his mind
to me, make him worship me, cling to me:
his dinghy, shelter from rough storms at sea,
so he'd want me all legal and church-signed:

true love winning, like in troubadours' songs.
But I'm just his instrument, his sharp tool
for cutting truth out of the hearts of fools.
To him, I'm just one servant in a throng.

So why shouldn't I take my quick farewell
with Billy, and curse Raven to darkest hell?

Captain James Raven Considers Kathleen Munro

I can read her mind like a children's book:
considering quitting our pirate trade
with this reluctant recruit we waylaid
when we overwhelmed his ship, just their cook

escaping, and me ordering the jade
to worm her way into this new man's heart,
and find out if he intends to depart
and have us chained in the Governor's stockade,

and from there to the gallows and a swing
into black eternity. For his soul
doesn't rejoice when we blast broadside holes
into ships we take from a distant king.

I fear she tires of our riotous life:
tempted to be a small, harmless man's wife.

The Pirate Kathleen Munro Further Vacillates About Leaving

Not so simple to simply walk away,
or rather, steal a dinghy and escape
on a fair sea breeze with Billy, and scrape
off this pirate life, and avoid the fray

of constant worry we'll all be captured
by the Governor's men and slowly hanged
after we've been battered, beaten, and banged
about: the dread end of our adventure.

If I leave with Billy, no guarantee
we'll elude the Raven and his sea curs—
who'd ravage and kill their own mothers—
to find a haven to live safe and free.

And do I want to run, when there's a chance
Raven might grace me with more than a glance?

Kathleen Munro Thinks of Miranda Iglesias

Aside from all else, there's the small matter
of Miranda, Raven's consort, the brains
of his pirate band; she hates me like chilblains.
So afraid I'd steal her man, she'd shatter

my head, rip out my heart, feed the red meat
to her hound. Hard to say if she'd let me be
if I ran away from our island with Billy,
or so afraid we'd find the Guvnor's fleet

and reveal their redoubt, she'd waylay us,
treat with us in a swift, brutal manner,
flay off our skin like an expert tanner,
then finish us off with a blunderbuss.

Safer if we could poison her secretly,
and while Raven's grieving take to the sea.

Miranda Iglesias, Consort of Captain Raven

If I ever scent that cunnie Kathleen
on him again, I'll cut off his pizzle
and burn it before him until it sizzles
and shrivels down to the size of a bean.

I told him, "It's me or no one for you,
and don't dare think you can get rid of me,
and shoot your seed like monkeys in a tree.
Believe me, you wee, randy toad, you'll rue

the instant you thought to have both that bitch
and me! I'm the brains of our pirate band,
working behind your bluster with my plans.
Stay on my safe side; you know I'm a witch.

I let you swagger and fret like a king,
but without me, your queen, you'd likely swing."

How Miranda Iglesias Became a Pirate

In public, my people were New Christians,
church converts, making the sign of the cross,
pretending to love the sick reek of pork.
While in private, we prayed to *Elohim,*

the true God. We kept kosher, kept the *Shabbat;*
but I confess, that yoke weighed heavily
on my shoulders, those rules burdening me,
to make me wish to be free, and to plot

my escape. I haunted the port's haven
for ships whose masts proudly flew the black flag,
or the other signs of buccaneer swag,
and made bold eyes at bold Captain Raven,

proved to him I wasn't a soft daughter,
but a wild girl, loving mayhem and slaughter.

How Miranda Iglesias Became a Pirate, II

My parents wept at my running away;
they cursed I was a blight, a mortal stain
in tradition-and Jesus-obsessed Spain
where we hid we were Jews, each night, each day:

It's why my forebears took a churchly name
like "Iglesias" two centuries ago,
when the Inquisition threatened to throw
us into hell's burning pit, for Jew-shame.

Now, I schemed to meet the pirate head-man;
when we talked, he was tranced by my midnight,
"Take me," eyes, the dirk I kept in plain sight,
all part of my ruthless, desperate plan

to make him see I was a necessary
intimate of his devil's coterie.

How Miranda Iglesias First Proved Her Mettle as a Pirate

Leading that wolf pack of a pirate crew,
I howled across flung-down ship-grappling ladders
and slashed my cutlass as blood boiled madder:
the fat merchantman's deck a gory stew.

Far from sobbing at taking lives, I roared
my joy to finally be free of chains,
of hiding—a Jew-mouse in Christian Spain—
and gladly pitched dead and living overboard.

Indeed, so fierce was my murderous lust
my mates backed away, in fear of my rage,
my fury a tiger bursting its cage,
shattering hard iron bars into rust.

Hell-hearted scum bowed to me, their new queen,
who'd lead them, with my plots and plans and schemes.

Miranda Iglesias, on Gaining the Attention of James Raven

Being bold in taking that caravel,
more ruthless than any of his male crew,
that pleased him in a woman, a Jew,
made him raise me up, for my lethal skill.

He was tranced like a mouse by an adder,
took me to his bed, or rather, I took him,
but let him think he had to toil to win
me, had to work to climb my Jacob's Ladder,

when I'd have been his for the mere asking.
Yet I couldn't let him see I was easy,
but had to be coaxed, jollied, was queasy,
and then the lascivious, languorous unmasking.

Ever since, I've been the queen of his heart,
though of late, he smiles at harlots and tarts.

Captain Raven Remembers His First and Only Slave Ship

How I detested that life-sucking knave,
my comfortable slave-purveying Father,
who'd brow-beaten and hit my poor mother
into a feverish, too early grave.

With no tears for her, he set me to learn
how to be a slave master on a slave ship,
to make sure no chattel escaped the whip,
or sought death and freedom over the stern.

Soon, I was scheming with those shackled souls,
on how to rise and take over the craft,
with a few other Jack Tars, fore and aft,
then sail to Africa's valleys and knolls

and release those cringing, starved, beaten men,
then sail the seas, raiding fat merchantmen.

James Raven Rationalizes Sending Captured Crewmen into Indentured Servitude

I tell myself the sentence ain't for life,
just a mere seven years of hard, healthy toil
working in the sun, tilling good, rich soil,
and even the chance to take a sweet wife.

At the end of their terms, generous shillings
for the work they've put in, plus the freedom
to make their way in the world, as free men
in the Colonies, without care or strings

to work their own land, or another trade:
many years of life and love before them,
of seeing their sons grow into fine men,
their daughters married, not slatternly jades.

But it's all to still my unquiet soul;
I've shattered lives I can never make whole.

Captain Raven Remembers His First Pirate Command

We vowed to raid cargo-heavy galleons
once we freed the souls in that slave-ship hold;
then some of those lads swore to make so bold
as to join our fierce pirate battalion.

We roved to take merchantmen ripe as plums,
make groaning ships-of-the-line deliver
their fat cargos, their crews all aquiver
to join us, or tossed overboard, for chum.

What freedom, to raise our black pirate flag,
knowing that honest crews all shat their britches,
feared us more than wolves, warlocks, and witches,
while we itched at the thought of so much swag.

That was the life, all exciting and new,
before this ghost started killing my crew.

Samuel Wallace Continues to Assassinate James Raven's Pirate Crew

I drive the Raven into an ague
of rage and terror: not safe even here
on his island lair and hideout, from where
he launches raids, turns the sea into a stew

of blood and unearths new pirate recruits
from trembling crews that don't desire a stroll
among sharks, while captured ships bob and roll,
his scurvy ranks swelling with knaves and brutes.

Though whispers burden the air like storm clouds:
an assassin stalks brazen as a ghost,
all along this be-damned pirate coast,
sending Raven's men off in winding shrouds.

He thought to outfox me here on the shore;
I'll bleed away his men, those gets of whores.

PART IV—THE GOVERNOR

Why the Governor Assumed His Posting

I couldn't refuse, though this is a fen
of snakes, spiders, and pirate-scum: the King
Himself stating it was just the posting
for a man like me, a leader of men.

He further flattered, I'd be doing him
and the realm he lazily rules, a service,
in ridding these islands of brigand-lice.
He promised funds to get rid of the vermin.

But like my wife, he lied: the two, paramours
and he withholding needed gold and troops,
since all he wants is to fox in my coop
with my wife: the harlot, his smiling whore.

When I return a failure, in two years' time,
he'll weary of her, the jade once more mine.

The Governor's Business Arrangements

I sailed away to this sweltering hell
to make my fortune, and not by the book,
no one over me to take a hard look
and report to the King and all his swells.

Nothing here but to sweat, sleep, whore, and take
a wolf-cut of every vessel's cargo,
my frigates maintaining an embargo
for any captain who tries to run and shake

the import duties every ship owes me,
as the King's lawful representative.
Besides, I need every shilling to live
more secure than to beg in penury.

All that keeps a man from going insane:
dreams of returning home with wealth and fame.

The Governor, on the Climate of the Islands

You'd think it too hot to even dream
of naked, sweaty flesh on snail-slick skin,
but it's all I think of, after I've been
at the King's business, air like choking steam.

At dusk, a breeze plays on flesh like soft hands
plucking at harp or lute strings, or lips blowing
expertly, to inflame lust, bodies knowing
what bodies are for in this sun-smudged land.

At night, serenades from the swaying trees,
and natives leap and howl about the flames
for my entertainment, except one plain
girl, skilled at bringing me to ecstasy.

I take revenge on my wife with the jade:
me, a man once clean as a new forged blade.

The Governor Thinks of His Mistress

A beauty she is not, no more to say,
but she has a way of holding herself.
And while her face is not the pure of Delft,
like Pamphleteer Wilkes, she can talk away

her visage with pleasant conversation,
and she's most inventive between the sheets
that groan all sweaty when we meet and meet:
just the antidote for my consternation

with those pirates that plague my nights and days,
who so far have evaded my stratagems,
but I'll crush those hell-bound fiends in the end,
then devote more time to her hooks and stays.

But I'll have to forget her once we part,
when I sail for England without the tart.

John Wilkes, for whom John Wilkes Booth, President Lincoln's assassin, was named, was an 18th century British political pamphleteer and reputed to be the greatest lady's man of his time. He was also incredibly ugly. Once he was asked how a man with his face could be such a success with the ladies. His reply? "Sir, give me half an hour and I can talk my face away."

Eliza Townes Thinks of Her Paramour, the Governor

I learned early that a quick wit becomes
a female more than a face like a dove,
that a tongue can make a man fall in love,
for beauty alone can grow so tiresome,

as to make her lover look elsewhere to burn,
unless a woman can make her man laugh
and praise overly the sword in his pants,
though it's so much work for such small return.

I've also thought a woman on her own
must look to her future security,
and hoard his gifts of generosity
to ease her life when she's old and alone.

When my fat little lordling sails away,
I'll think not of men the rest of my days.

The Governor Explains Why He Hasn't Sent Troops to Take the Pirate Stronghold

The King, that fat-sloven, dawdles to send
the troops I require to take Raven's stronghold-
island, so the freebooter-rat makes bold
to taunt me, as if there will be no end

to his merchantman-boarding butcher-ways.
My spies tell me he swaggered and strutted
even as he cringed from the wraith that gutted
his crew like gasping marlins and stingrays.

But now that he's sought sanctuary on shore
from the ghost haunting the ship his men took,
again he prances in his sheltered nook,
assured of his safety from the King's law.

If only I had—my vile nemesis—
men enough, you'd be a fly in my fist.

PART V—CAPTURE

Kathleen Munro Changes Her Mind About the Pirate Life

I've grown weary of pirate butchery,
of merchantmen decks slippery with blood,
of sending good men to ocean-floor mud,
of living for greed, grog, and savagery.

I look at Billy now, and want a life
of not searching the horizon for
the Governor's avenging men o' war,
and want to go to bed without a knife

invisibly stabbing my trembling heart,
beating so I can't sleep, but lie here
waiting for the dead I made, to appear
and kill me: nothing but a vicious tart.

I want to be with Billy, on dry land,
in a safe life beyond the sea's quicksand.

The Governor, Ready to Attack the Pirate Stronghold

At last, I've been given the men I need
from our formerly miserly Monarch,
who now sends me soldiers ample as lark
song, his order: to slay the scum with speed.

As if dispatching them were effortless,
and required no surveillance, no planning,
no assessment of their numbers or scanning
for their ambuscades, armories, and fortress.

"King" another name for Divinity,
Who has but to think something to make it
so, unconcerned by life's eternal shit:
even more perfect than the Trinity.

If I botch any of His sacred commands,
the King will wash me from His holy hands.

Billy Butcher and Kathleen Munro Escape

I hid a dinghy in the shoaled inlet:
from seaward, the cliffs sheer as isinglass;
from the land, just one all-but-hidden path
through swamps, quicksand, and Spanish bayonet.

A path only I knew well enough to trust
my feet and life to. While the others snored,
Kath and I quietly reaped all we'd stored
and crept off to that cove, silent as dust,

terrified we'd make a noise, and they'd wake
and hunt us down, relentless as mastiffs,
and rip us up before we'd reach the cliffs,
or like savages, impale us with stakes.

Finally, we stole our way to the beach,
praying to sail and row beyond their reach.

The Governor Deploys His Forces Against the Pirate Stronghold

We'll wait for the darkest hour of the night,
when the hell-bound rats are all drunk and asleep,
all of them lying in an orgy-heap,
farting and snoring that all's well and right.

When they're still as the graves they'll soon lie in,
we'll creep up, slit throats, but be sure to take
their leader, this Raven, alive, to make
a dancing-gallows example of him,

so new recruits won't be tempted to ply
the pirate trade, and put honest galleons
and crews at risk from thieving battalions.
We'll make him do a scaffold jig, up high.

Once his neck's snapped, he's bound for the gibbet;
his carcass pecked, 'til nothing's left of it.

Too Late, Pirate James Raven Discovers the Desertion of Billy Butcher and Kathleen Munro

If we weren't pinned down by Lobsterbacks
ambushing us out of false dawn's dank mists,
drooling to drag us off by manacled wrists
and hang us after their coward-attack,

I'd be after Butcher and bitch-Kathleen:
Miranda warned me they were deceitful
as mangy curs that gorge themselves 'til full
before they turn on masters, mad with spleen.

I should've listened to her. But Butcher?
All I saw was the son I never had.
And Munro? I thought her docile and sad.
But now they've eluded their slaughter

by stealing sacks of gold coins mine by right,
and slinking off with dawn's accusing light.

Captured, James Raven Voices His Regrets

What regrets gnaw at me the most? Not that
I didn't crush Butcher and his whore Munro
like bugs before they stole my lovely gold,
the dirty, thieving, double-dealing rats.

But that I let pirate greed cloud my intent
to free all the bound dupes of all slave ships:
other men's suffering nothing but a quip
to slave-sellers, men of sulphurous scent,

who saw their brothers as mere merchandise
made to savor the lash's bitter feast,
to stoop at toil without rest or release,
'til tossed under the dirt in a trice,

to molder far from their own land and kin,
this new world to them, mere pain to the brim.

PART VI—HELL AT COCK'S CROW

The Governor, Before the Execution of James Raven

Had I noose-danced him to hell at cock's crow,
I'd have been quietly rid of the fool
before he became a martyr and tool
for factions to whom the King is opposed.

But the mob demands a theatrical,
a grand performance to entertain them,
and hawkers require a steady income
from ale and meat pies; plus, strolling minstrels

must sweeten their curdling tales in broadsides
of bold and gallant Captain James Raven,
who was the Beelzebub of this Eden:
a merchantman-destroying homicide.

So he'll swing at noon, with pretty sluts pressed
forward: his solace, their unbodiced breasts.

James Raven Addresses the Vicar at His Hanging

I'll not repent, will not go in a whimper,
as docile as a cringing mongrel wagging
its tail after yet another slagging
from its master's fists and kicks, the cur's simpers

merely making its god more and more cruel.
Repent? To the Lord, who doesn't exist?
To the corporations that owned the ships
we took? They play the rest of us for fools,

tilting the game, without a by-your-leave,
while ordinary sods bow to these lords
as if they own the whole world, aboveboard,
and charge us a fee for the air we breathe.

The only ones I'll apologize to?
The sailors too simple to join our crews.

James Raven's Final Words to the Hangman

Don't muck up my death, you son of a whore,
but from your smirk, I see you'll make me dance
for the mob's amusement; you'll have me prance
and gag and turn tar-black while the sods roar

their joy at another bugger's expense,
while I shit myself, my jism flying
like a filthy fountain at my dying.
Here, take coins for your mercy's recompense

in my hope I'll go in a finger-snap,
my neck broken in the blink of an eye,
so that I won't even know that I've died,
but gone to the land beyond any map:

though I can see you're the Governor's pet,
and will serve him with murderous etiquette.

The Hangman Converses with James Raven on the Scaffold

The Governor's paid me a handsomer purse
to make sure your dying is slow as some rakes
can draw out strumpets' delights in their aches
and moans, until in their passion they claw, curse

and yowl for release in lust-filled blatherings,
like cannons splattering into the Boyne.
So why should I accept your dribbling coins
and risk the Governor's wrathful batterings?

Besides, the crowd roars for you to produce
a show, a performance they can jeer for,
to help them forget their lives are so poor,
while you dance, jigged by your hempen noose.

And if I don't give them what they expect,
you know I'll be dancing and kicking next.

Samuel Wallace at the Hanging of James Raven

I thought I'd be buoyed by a vengeful delight
to watch him dance and stagger in mid-air;
like the rest of the mob, I'd shout and jeer
his bucking and jerks, a satisfying sight.

I thought I'd be cheering for my revenge
for Raven forcing my comrades to choose
between joining his scurvy, hell-bound crew
or be tossed off the plank's teetering edge

into the maws of waiting, circling sharks,
teeth heartless as the scimitars of Moors,
not a chance for those lads to swim to shore,
while pirates mocked at such fine, jolly larks.

But I find myself standing solemn and still,
unseemly to joy at the hangman's skill.

Miranda Iglesias, in the Crowd at James Raven's Hanging

Dear James, I've come to bid you sad farewell,
one face that's not a mask of cruel delight
or an oh-so-sanctified sneer to smite
you into pitiless, eternal hell.

We'd a good, long run, as a pirate pair,
earned and tossed away many a fortune
from merchantmen fat as the hunter's moon,
turned the sea red, but treated our crew fair.

We had a lovely time, as well, in bed,
you taught me all the dance steps of pleasure,
a gift exceeding our pirate treasure:
the memory still floats and soars in my head.

'Til we meet once more above or below,
I'll have to make do with our bags of gold.

The Governor to His Lieutenant, at the Hanging of James Raven

Cast your eyes on that copper-tressed beauty,
silent amid the baying rabble: still
as an oak standing by a windless rill.
The strumpet's doing her final duty

of love to that rogue upon the scaffold.
Discreet as a vicar, escort her here;
together we'll get her to confess where
they buried their murderous pirate gold.

When we've finished with her, do with the jade
as you please, then dispose of the harlot
in any ruthless fashion you see fit,
so long as she's silent as an old grave.

But oh, I'd have her for my concubine,
though beauty can mask a poisonous vine.

Miranda Iglesias Tries to Escape from the Governor's Henchman

They must've took me for a wall-eyed hag,
not to have observed the Governor's man—
obvious as a full sailed catamaran—
who'd knife-tickle me for my treasure bags.

So I started drifting back in the crowd,
picking the ground where I'd launch my attack
and plunge my dagger in his dirty back:
I'd be silent as the gauze of a shroud.

"Come out, dearie," he tried to soothe, as if
taunting a starved hound with a meaty bone,
only to switch it for a granite stone.
All the time I floated toward the cliff,

but didn't reckon on his underlings,
who closed on me, silent, on demon-wings.

Taken Prisoner by the Governor, Miranda Iglesias Makes the Best of Things

I had to play a most convincing part:
of withholding where James and I had hidden
our sacks of hard-earned pirate gold and gems
before I'd tearfully break down and impart

where we'd buried them, all the while pleading
with my breasting-sighs for him to spare me,
for, if not his consort, then as a slavey
he could use for his pleasure, like a king.

All the while I'd be plotting my escape
with my one remaining sack of stashed loot,
and scrape off this hole, like shit from my boot,
to live without care in a kinder place.

I knew the Governor wanted me dead,
but my tears softened the dull fucker's head.

Miranda Iglesias Plans Her Escape

I was such a compliant consort,
the Governor let me flutter like a quail
over each inch of his soft island jail,
thinking me his prisoner. I'd report

back: spying on possible rebellions
he could put down, as the King's head man
before sailing home for civil London,
not this seething rat's nest of a fen.

I feared he'd order my execution
before he'd go, afraid I'd take once more
to the buccaneer trade, become a whore
of havoc, and foment revolution.

On my rambles, I hatched schemes of freedom,
stole the heart of a gullible captain.

Miranda Iglesias Rids Herself of the Governor

Exquisite poison proved to be my friend,
my escape from his soft island prison.
The potion in my hand caused such a frission,
the obeah woman-crone had to bend

my fingers into a ball, to keep me
from dropping the vial before the tincture
could perform its deadly, freeing task, sure
as blue waves lapping the strand from the sea.

The false-pleasant tasting ooze put him down
without a croak or groan; it made him look
as if the benevolent hand of God took
him to Paradise, where he'd wear a crown.

To heaven or hell, I didn't care which,
or toss the randy boar into a ditch.

EPILOGUE—ON THE SEA AND BEYOND

Billy Butcher and Kathleen Munro, on the Sea

I scan the sea, no pirate man o' war
looms like a death-flame dragon in pursuit,
for our sneaking off with our share of the loot
from the others: the thieving spawn of whores.

Should Raven's ship find and run us to ground
he'll bloody his sword edge against my head
for leaving without leave, then leave me dead,
and feed Kathleen to his infernal hounds:

his men, I mean, at their dirty pleasure;
finished, she'll be a moaning, broken mess,
mangled and torn by their brutal caress,
praying to be quickly killed by the curs.

I fear our luck is too fickle to hold,
but our sail bellies; wind bellows, "Be bold!"

Miranda Iglesias Returns to the Pirate Life

Once on board the ship that helped me elude
the island of the Governor's soft restraint,
easy to goad the men to rise against
their captain, and make me head of that crew,

then convince them the pirate life was one
they longed to follow, sea winds caressing
their faces like lovers, fat ships a blessing
of gold, bellies full, the joy of the big guns

pounding in broadsides, to shatter ship's keels
and reduce all on board to pleading tears,
Jack Tars terrified by their greatest fears:
that sharks would rip them for blood-bathed meals.

"We'll raven the sea like wolves!" I promised,
my bared breasts pledging each lad's dreams of bliss.

Billy Butcher and Kathleen Munro Make Landfall

We've fetched up on an isolated coast
of the Colonies, I think: soil rich and black
as good blood pudding. I've put up a shack,
started to clear and plow land to act as host

for the seeds I've bartered from the savages;
Kathleen's sweet belly begins to grow plump
with the child who'll gambol, play, and jump
without a care from freebooter ravages

I took part in to save my frightened ass
when pirates attacked us with shot and shell,
and sent my shipmates to a watery hell.
Now Kathleen and me have fled, bold and fast.

It's an honest life we look forward to,
not one of murder in the devil's crew.

Kathleen Munro, After the Birth of Her and Billy's Butcher Son

I thought I'd leave Billy once the bairn came,
but looking down now at its suckling face,
my milk a holy stream, no other place
I'd want to be: Henry will be his name.

Such a dear wee head and soft lips on him,
such tiny, insistent gripping fingers,
his fat legs kicking delight that lingers
past my feeding his belly to the brim.

And here's Billy staring down in surprise,
amazed we're both part of a family,
that such a grand lad came from him and me.
And just look at his perfect little eyes!

As for the pirate life I thought I'd miss,
I'd rather one sweet-as-cream baby-kiss.

Billy Butcher, Five Years After His Pirate Adventures Have Ended

I've never stopped listening, looking around
for my former companions-in-slaughter,
while Kathleen gave me a sweet, wee daughter
after our son, and we grew crops in good ground.

Then a traveler, who sojourned one night,
informed us Captain Raven had been stretched
some years back, his crew similarly vexed
except the pretty Spaniard, who took flight:

witch-Miranda: she rules a pirate ship
that terrorizes the isles of the Main,
sending them nightmares all over again,
when she raids and gives the Navy the slip.

Little chance we'll wake to her pirate dirk,
but still we dream of her murderous smirk

Miranda Iglesias Has the Last Word

The Main was getting too hot for our trade,
the Navy seeming to know where we'd hit
and when, so best to sail north for a bit,
to the Colonies, not prepared for a raid

to its long, inviting, unshielded shore.
Besides, I know where Billy and slut Kathleen
are hiding on that peaceful and bright green
coast, farming in the wilderness: the whore

dropping a son and daughter to Billy,
the tiny darlings of their traitor-eyes
we could take hostage with rapier-surprise,
and demand their sire and dam's loyalty.

But no, let them scratch at their meager soil,
grow old and bitter with unending toil.

About the Author

Robert Cooperman grew up on the not-so-mean streets of Brooklyn and went to grad school in Denver, Colorado. He holds a Ph.D. in English, with a joint concentration in Creative Writing and 19th Century British Literature from the University of Denver. While his first two loves were basketball and the Grateful Dead, he's the author of over 20 poetry collections, most recently, *Bearing the Body of Hector Home* (FutureCycle Press), a retelling of the killing of the Trojan hero Hector and his burial rites, toward the end of *The Iliad*. *Draft Board Blues* was named one of Ten Great Books by a Colorado Author for 2017, by *Westword Magazine*. *In the Colorado Gold Fever Mountains* won the Colorado Book Award for Poetry for 2000, and *The Widow's Burden* was runner-up for the Willa Award, from Women Writing the West, in 2001. Other recent collections include *City Hat Frame Factory* and *A Nightmare on Horse Back,* both from Kelsay Books.

After living and teaching in Athens, GA, Bowling Green, OH, and Baltimore, Cooperman is happily back in Denver, and living with his wife Beth.

www.ingramcontent.com/pod-product-compliance
Lightning Source LLC
Chambersburg PA
CBHW030053170426
43197CB00010B/1508